Praise for *Rev Your Résumé*

Andrea hits the nail on the head. This little book has the BIG idea that will help you take your career to the next level. Before you take one more step in your job search, read this book and follow its guidance.

-Lee B. Salz, sales management strategist, author of the award-winning book, *Soar Despite Your Dodo Sales Manager*

Rev Your Résumé shows job seekers how to land their ideal job fast! Ms. Sittig-Rolf uses very simple and compelling stories and examples to demonstrate how to apply proven selling skills to the job search. Her approach has a proven track record and every job seeker should start using her advice today.

-Jeanette Nyden, J.D., author of *Negotiation Rules! A Practical Approach to Big Deal Negotiation*

I get résumés weekly from job seekers because I am so well connected in my community. Their résumés are usually a mess and don't represent the individuals well. They have no idea how to find a job, let alone their dream job. Andrea's book is just what they need. From now on I am going to respond to their emails with a link to purchase her book.

-Alice R. Heiman, President, Alice Heiman LLC

Revolutionize, Revitalize & Rev Your Résumé

Create Your Accomplishments Portfolio &
Land Your Dream Job

Andrea Sittig-Rolf

ASPATORE

Mat #40929729

ASPATORE

Aspatore Books, a Thomson Reuters business, exclusively publishes C-Level executives (CEO, CFO, CTO, CMO, Partner) from the world's most respected companies and law firms. C-Level Business Intelligence™, as conceptualized and developed by Aspatore Books, provides professionals of all levels with proven business intelligence from industry insiders—direct and unfiltered insight from those who know it best—as opposed to third-party accounts offered by unknown authors and analysts. Aspatore Books is committed to publishing an innovative line of business and legal books, those which lay forth principles and offer insights that, when employed, can have a direct financial impact on the reader's business objectives, whatever they may be. In essence, Aspatore publishes critical tools for all business professionals.

CONTENTS

Acknowledgments

The purpose of writing this book is to share the successful job search and interview scheduling techniques that have evolved as a result of practicing them myself and teaching them to others throughout my career as a sales professional since 1991 and small business owner since 2002.

In addition to my siblings Katy, Janet, and Carl, and my husband Brian, who have always been extremely supportive, I want to thank you for investing in a copy of this book, particularly at a time when money might be tight. I was inspired to write this book based on my own personal experience of being in your shoes and either wanting a better job, or just needing a job period. I was inspired to write this book *now* because of what's happening with our economy and because of the 10% unemployment rate, the highest we've seen in 26 years. I want to do my part to help Americans get back to work!

My hope for you is that as a result of putting these tactics and strategies into practice, you will land your dream job. My plan is to inspire and motivate you as you continue your job search!

Introduction

Many years ago, I found myself in quite a predicament. I managed to accumulate thousands of dollars of debt and was living paycheck to paycheck, making minimum payments on credit cards and not making a dent in the debt I owed. Although I had a good-paying job at the time, it wasn't enough to get ahead of my debt. I decided to work with a debt consolidation firm, which helped me form a six-year plan to pay off my debt; but mind you, the six-year plan was based on the debt I had at the time and didn't take into consideration any other debt I might incur while paying off the current debt!

After carefully considering my situation, and dreading the next six years I had in front of me to pay off my debt, I began to ponder other ways to get out of debt faster. Why not, I thought, get a better-paying job, that would allow me to pay off the debt sooner than six years? After all, if I was making more money, I could make bigger payments on the debt and put something towards principle each month as well, cutting the debt down to size even faster.

IT WORKED! Several short months after making this decision and forming a new plan to get a better paying job, I landed a new job that not only paid double the salary of my previous one, but included additional commissions and bonuses as well! Instead of paying off the debt in six years, I paid it off in SIX MONTHS!

How did I do it? What was my secret weapon? Can you do it too? I'll answer the last question first...YES YOU CAN! Keep reading....

Now more than ever, employers are bombarded with standard, boring, one-page résumés, and they're buried in e-mail and electronic and video résumés as well. If you're going to get not just a job, but a better-paying job, you have to stand out in the crowd of résumés that your potential employers are getting every day. It's no longer effective in this economy to do the same old same old and expect to land a good job. If you want to rise to the top, you have to show how and why you're different than every other candidate interviewing for the same job. Your potential employer has to see you shine and rise above the potential hundreds of other applicants they are in contact with every day.

Think you don't have enough experience? Think you haven't accomplished anything worthy of sharing? Think you're not special enough and don't have any gifts to offer an employer, and that they wouldn't be absolutely thrilled to have you work for them? WRONG! You have all of these things: experience, accomplishments, and gifts. It's just a matter of organizing them in such a way that showcases the best of your abilities and the bottom-line results you can create for a future employer based on what you've done in the past. Trust me, if you don't feel confident now that your accomplishments are good enough to get that job you really want, you WILL after doing this exercise, which is just one of the many benefits of doing this activity. The increased confidence you'll feel is also something that will help you interview better. Employers will notice your confidence, which is exactly what they want to see when considering a candidate for employment. At the end of this book, you'll have your own secret weapon, and such confidence to present it to potential employers that you may just find yourself in a bidding war between companies that want to hire you, and you'll have the tough, but welcomed, decision on which job to take!

Ready to know what I did to get a better, higher-paying job that allowed me to pay off six years of debt in six months? How about how I was able to negotiate an additional $25,000 in annual salary than was allocated for yet another job? Or how I was able to negotiate a signing bonus at another job? I'm going to show you the original template I created so you can do exactly what I did and create your very own

Accomplishments Portfolio that will *Revolutionize, Revitalize, and Rev Up Your Résumé* and empower you to finally land your dream job!

Warning: This book is not for the faint of heart or the pathologically humble. You are going to learn how to create what is essentially a "brag book." It may be a more aggressive approach than you've been willing to take in the past, but if you've picked up this book, chances are you need to try something different, a new approach that will finally get you results. You will, at times while reading this book, think, "Wow, this woman sure does think highly of herself!" Well, you're right. And you will also think highly of yourself once you've created your very own Accomplishments Portfolio. As I mentioned, a nice side effect of compiling your Accomplishments Portfolio is the confidence you'll feel once it's complete. Trust me, employers would rather see confidence, even if it is "extreme," in a job applicant than uncertainty or insecurity. So, if you're willing to take this journey with me now, to step up and be ready to think highly of yourself and be willing to share your gifts and accomplishments with others to land your dream job, read on…

1

Creating Your "Ideal Job Profile"

How many times have you actually thought about what your ideal job is, versus just finding the next potential employer you think might be willing to hire you? Think about it. Think about how your life would change if you spent your days working in an ideal job. Think about what that dream job would look like. What would make it ideal? What are the parameters of, or formula for, your dream job? What size company is it? How many employees do they have? How much do they do in revenue each year? Who are their clients? What is their product or service? How many locations do they have? How do they go to market (i.e., direct versus indirect sales, retail, channel sales, etc.)? How much money do you make each year working in your dream job? These are all questions that should be considered when defining your dream job. They will also lead to certain industries or specific vertical markets that will make excellent employer prospects for you based on the nature of their industry or business.

In my previous sales books, I talk about defining your ICP, or "Ideal Client Profile," that, when translated for the job seeker, allows you to focus only on those potential employers who fit your Ideal Job Profile, which for our purposes we might call the IJP. This also allows you to quickly identify someone who is not an ideal employer and quickly move on to someone who is. Think about how much more effective you could be in attracting ideal employers when you're no longer wasting time with employers who aren't the best fit for what you do anyway, for whatever reason. It took me two years after starting my business to realize the difference between ideal clients and non-ideal clients. When I first started the company and began promoting The Blitz Experience, our activity-based new business development program, I initially focused on any company, no matter what size, that had a sales team of at least three people. Without knowing it, that is how I was defining my ICP: companies that had a sales team of at least three people. That's it—no other factors were taken into consideration. This approach forced me to "start over" not only each month, but literally each day to determine where my next paycheck was coming from, since there was often no potential for any future business with that client. And believe me, that's no way to live! I was successful at finding clients, but I was running myself ragged because they were mostly small, one-time clients.

Two years after starting my business, I stumbled onto an account that had a large sales team in the form of a "dealer network." It was a commercial furniture manufacturing company that went to market not through a direct sales channel, but through manufacture rep companies and dealers across the country that sold their products to the end user. Lo and behold, I had hit the mother lode and didn't even know it! It started small, with a Blitz Experience program here and there, but soon word got out and I actually had to hire other "Blitz Masters" (sales trainers) just to meet the demand that was created for the program within their dealer network! The next client I landed had a similar profile, except they were a major software manufacturing company. They too went to market not through a direct sales channel, but through a dealer network. Similar to the commercial furnishings company, this client began with two Blitz Experience programs with a dealer in North Carolina, and when the program was so successful at that location, I received an e-mail from the general manager telling me he wanted to roll out the program to the remaining 300 sales reps in eight other cities. That single project generated more revenue for my company than all of the revenue generated in the previous two years combined!

Finally, after two years, I had begun to get the hang of it. I got to thinking, "Hmmm, what is it about these two clients that is so different from the other clients I have been working with?" That's when I decided to create a formal process to determine my ICP. First, by defining the ideal client and then pursuing only those prospects that fit the ICP, I would have an entire business focused on only the best of the best. I would also learn to quickly identify who fit the ICP and who did not so I could move on quickly in situations where a prospect was not ideal according to the profile. I thought, "Why not turn the tables on this whole sales game? Why does it have to be that the client gets to choose whether to work with my company? Why can't I choose which clients I want to work with?" I actually increased my revenue by eight and a half times my average just by deciding what it was about these two new accounts that made them so lucrative for my business.

What came next, after defining my ICP, was the realization that by nature of certain industries, there was an automatic fit with my ICP. For example, I soon realized that commercial office furniture and software manufacturing companies were both excellent vertical markets because of the way they went to market through dealer networks, indicating that the same type of opportunity existed because of these particular industries and the way they traditionally go to market. After selecting other commercial office furniture and software manufacturing companies, the only other determining factor was their size. If they were a small manufacturing company and only had a handful of dealers, it was not something I would pursue. However, if they were a large company with an extensive dealer network, it was something I would pursue.

I also soon realized that large companies that sold directly to their clients, rather than going through a sales channel methodology, were great prospects for The Blitz Experience. It made sense to pilot the program at one office and then, with proven success, roll it out to the entire company. This tactic allowed me to sell the program just once to the key decision-makers at large organizations and then simply fulfill Blitz orders once the word spread and salespeople as well as sales managers in the organization began to hear about the success of the Blitz program in other departments.

Much of what I did here can easily translate to the job seeker. After all, in this case, *you* are the product to sell, so to speak, so applying sales techniques and concepts to the job search process isn't that much of a stretch! What may be a stretch, out of your comfort zone anyway, is the idea of approaching companies that aren't necessarily hiring, and propose that they hire you for a job you've created for yourself, and ultimately for them. This concept is really based on the idea that, when looking for a job, you are truly a salesperson with something to sell, and that is the idea that you would be an asset to any organization based on a job description you've come up with on your own.

What are the benefits of this approach? How about no competition? What about naming your salary? How about just being able to do something you love every day?

If you've created a job that doesn't already exist, think about it: no one else knows about it, so no one else will be applying for it...you are the only job applicant for whatever job it is you create! Would naming your own salary be a benefit? Uhh, yeah it would! This is where really understanding the sales process and selling your value to an organization becomes so important. If the job doesn't already exist, you can propose a salary based on the value you think it's worth. If it's a high salary, you'll have to have your ducks in a row to justify what you're asking, but that's all part of what you'll learn here, especially if you've had no exposure to sales in the past. Finally, just getting to do what you love every day is a huge benefit and not one you can even put a price on.

As I mentioned, this approach requires understanding some basic sales techniques so that you can apply them to your job search. And the next step, after determining your IJP and before making your interview-setting calls, is to review how to find key online resources to keep your pipeline full of potential employer leads.

An invaluable resource I have found online while seeking employment is Giga Alerts (formerly known as Google Alerts), at www.gigaalert.com. Giga Alerts are e-mail updates of the latest relevant Google results (Web, news, etc.) based on your choice of query or topic. Giga Alerts allow you to automatically receive information related to potential employers, their customers, their competitors, and other information to help generate qualified job leads and arm you with the market intelligence you need to have compelling conversations with potential employers, showing them you've done your homework before scheduling the interview. Some handy uses of Giga Alerts include:

- Monitoring a developing news story
- Learning about companies that are hiring
- Learning about mergers and acquisitions
- Getting the latest on job and career fairs and where they're being held
- Keeping current on a competitor or industry
- Getting the latest on a celebrity or event
- Keeping tabs on your favorite sports teams

Think about trigger events in your industry or expertise that could be used as Giga Alerts. Is the hiring of a specific type of personnel something that would be a trigger event for a job lead for you? Of course! What about being in the know of where job/career fairs are being held? Would that be helpful? What about a company that is moving? Are mergers and acquisitions good job leads for you? Chances are, yes, as often these types of deals can create new jobs. Consider creating Giga Alerts based on job titles so that when a particular job is announced online, you'll receive that data immediately and can respond. All of these triggers can be created as a Giga Alert and notify you on a regular basis about the goings-on in the marketplace and can be a constant source of job leads for you. And the best part is…it's FREE!

In my business, for example, it is important to know which companies have a vice president of sales, since they are typically the decision-maker in regards to sales training and new business development, and a vice president level indicates a certain size company that would fit my ICP. Also, strategic alliances indicate the "dealer network" format that fits my ICP. I receive press release e-mails each day from Google that contain the words "vice president of sales" and "strategic alliance." Since the press release usually has to do with the hiring or promotion of a vice president of sales or the forming of a new strategic alliance, that tells me the particular company is growing and has budget available in their sales department. It also gives me the name of my contact, the vice president of sales, or the person in charge of the strategic alliance.

Another terrific online resource is www.nationalcareerfairs.com, which allows you to browse career fairs by region.

If you're not yet a member of LinkedIn, an online network of more than 50 million experienced professionals from around the world, you should be. It is another fantastic free resource, and when you join, you create a profile that summarizes your professional accomplishments. Your profile helps you find and be found by former colleagues, clients, partners, and potential employers. You can add more connections by inviting trusted contacts to join LinkedIn and connect to you. Your network consists of your connections, your connections' connections, and the people they know, linking you to thousands of qualified professionals.

LinkedIn is an amazing tool. Through your network, you can:

- Find potential clients, service providers, subject experts, and partners who come recommended
- Be found for business opportunities and/or employment
- Search for great jobs
- Discover inside connections that can help you land jobs
- Get introduced to other professionals through the people you know

I highly recommended you drop everything and join now if you're not already a member: www.linkedin.com.

Additionally, here are some fantastic websites to assist with job hunting and career development.

- www.twitterjobsearch.com
- www.indeed.com
- www.glassdoor.com
- www.visualcv.com
- www.bls.gov
- www.conference-board.org
- www.wantedtech.com

Once you have found great leads using the above-mentioned resources, be sure to conduct the appropriate research before contacting the potential employer in order to sound educated on the employer's business during that first important conversation leading up to the job interview. Keep in mind that there is such a thing as "too much research," meaning you use research as an excuse not to get on the phone and make the calls you know you need to make! Try not to spend more than about five minutes researching each prospective employer. Remember, your purpose in the first phone call is to just get the interview. You will have the opportunity to "sell yourself" later when you meet with the employer face to face.

One last lead generation technique I'll share is one I discovered by accident. Several years ago, I was in Louisville, Kentucky, tagging along on a business trip with my husband. While he participated in workshops at the conference he was attending, I hung out in the lobby of the hotel and worked on the manuscript for my book called *The Seven Keys to Effective Business-to-Business Appointment Setting: Unlock Your Sales Potential* (Aspatore Books, 2006). One day, while typing away on my laptop, I overheard a conversation between a couple of salespeople who were attending a sales conference of a high-tech company. They were salespeople for a major software company that was a channel partner of the company sponsoring the event. I decided to make small talk. After chatting for a few minutes, one of the salespeople asked me what I did for a living. I explained that I created The Blitz Experience activity-based sales training program designed to empower salespeople to schedule appointments with qualified prospects the day of the training, resulting in a pipeline full of new opportunities at the end of the day. As it turns out, the salesperson I was talking to was often involved in "national call-out days" put on by his company to introduce the latest version of their software to the market. He was excited about what I was telling him about The Blitz Experience and said that, as a salesperson, he would appreciate any guidance on how to be more effective when scheduling appointments with new prospects when introducing the newest version of his software. We exchanged business cards, and when I returned home from the trip, I sent him some information about The Blitz Experience to share with the executives at his company. After receiving the information I sent, we exchanged e-mail a few times and then, lo and behold, I received an e-mail from the assistant of the vice president of marketing asking me for a meeting to discuss how I could help them make their national call-out days more effective! The moral of the story and this non-traditional lead generation technique? Hang out in hotel lobbies where conferences relative to your industry or job expertise are being held, and strike up a conversation with the people there!

2

Writing a Compelling Cover Letter and Résumé

Besides the Accomplishments Portfolio itself, the cover letter is your opportunity to make a great first impression. Often the cover letter will determine whether a prospective employer takes the time to read through the rest of your portfolio, so you want to be sure it's powerful and gets their attention.

Contrary to popular belief, the cover letter should be more about the results you've created at previous jobs than simply reciting back to the prospective employer the wording you picked up on their Web site about a particular job requisition. Although you want to include some of that language, they're going to care more about what qualifies you for the job, and what results you've created at other jobs, than your ability to copy and paste from their Web site.

Additionally, in the situation where you're not applying for an existing job, but rather creating and proposing one to a prospective employer, your cover letter will only be able to speak to results you've created previously, since there is no public job requisition for the job you're proposing.

By way of example, I'm providing the actual cover letter and my personal (updated) résumé I included in my Accomplishments Portfolio that helped me land a job that paid double the salary of my previous job. Using this same format, another cover letter helped me secure an additional $25,000 in annual salary than was initially allocated for that particular job. Finally, still using this same format, for yet another job, I was able to secure a signing bonus!

Note that the components of the cover letter comprise:

- Testimonial from former employer, customer, or colleague at the top, centered, before the date
- Introduction and purpose of contacting the prospective employer
- Information about experience that has prepared you for the job you're seeking and results you've created for former employers you could create for them (This section should share a lot of benefits to the prospective employer for hiring you. It should be two to three paragraphs in length.)
- Education
- Closing of letter indicating you will call on a specific date, about ten days from mailing it, to inquire about scheduling an interview (Versus the more traditional approach of "Please contact me to schedule an interview.")

"Andrea Sittig is clear, focused, and innovative in her approach. Her commitment to providing solutions that work benefits all. I completely respect, trust, and admire Andrea. She is a rare gem and an asset to represent any organization."
- Contact Name, Company Name

May 24, 1999

ABC Communications Company
123 Main Street
Any town, USA 10101

Dear Bob,

My name is Andrea Sittig. I am currently an Account Manager with Lucent Technologies in Seattle, Washington. As you may know, our Small Business Division has just been sold. Although the new company will make competitive offers to keep its employees, I have decided to look for other, more challenging opportunities within the telecommunications arena.

I am very interested in the Area Sales Manager position you have available for your Seattle, Washington, location.

My eight years of sales experience with seven years of telecommunications sales has extensively prepared me for sales management. I have a proven track record of success in both new business development and customer retention. I have worked independently through the administrative and sales process, utilizing various computer programs to process orders and conduct other business, along with working with a complex order process. In my current position as Account Manager for Lucent Technologies, I am responsible for assuring quality in all customer activities as well as a $1,020,000 annual quota.

Furthermore, I have provided sales forecast reports weekly and monthly. I have designed several Market Coverage Action Plans as well as Territory Coverage Plans in both my new acquisition and customer development roles at Lucent Technologies. I have also been responsible for settling billing issues for both cash paying customers and third part leasing customers, as well as working to resolve post-warranty and maintenance issues and scheduling conflicts with technicians, system consultants, and network service providers.

I have also had five years of experience selling and training end users on a service-provided voicemail service (Voice-Tel) when voicemail was a brand new technology. As a consistent top performer for Voice-Tel, I was commissioned to open the Anchorage, Alaska, territory with regular travel over a six-month period.

I am diversely networked in Seattle. I have lived here for eight years and in that time have developed many business contacts, including sales professionals, management personnel, chief executive officers, and presidents of companies of all industries. Because I have a tight network of business associates, hiring and development of sales personnel would be a welcomed challenge.

Finally, I have a Bachelor of Arts degree in psychology from Southwest Texas State University, May of 1991.

I will call you June 3 to inquire about scheduling an interview, but feel free to contact me sooner.

Sincerely,

Andrea Sittig

ANDREA SITTIG-ROLF

P.O. Box 2423 ♦ Redmond, Washington 98073
(206) 769-4886 ♦ info@sittiginc.com

*"Ms. Sittig is a highly enthusiastic missionary-for-business
resource. If you are looking to find and blast open doors of
opportunity to profitable relationships, she knows how!"*
- Contact Name, Company Name

PROFESSIONAL SUMMARY

A seasoned Entrepreneur, Sales Executive, Author, and Public Speaker
with practical experience in a diverse range of new business
development and sales methodologies, including business writing,
marketing, team-building, and sales team training. Demonstrated
ability to build two businesses simultaneously with exponential
revenue growth each year.

CAREER EXPERIENCE

SITTIG INCORPORATED, Redmond, Washington
2002–Present
President and CEO
www.sittiginc.com

Founded the company, transforming an idea into a successful sales
training organization. Provide clients with sales training as well as lead
generation and development on both a retainer and project basis.

- 2008. Published *Power Referrals: The Ambassador Method for
  Empowering Others to Promote Your Business and Do the Selling for
  You* (McGraw-Hill, 2008).

- 2007. Invited to be a content provider for CanDoGo, a performance enhancement Web site designed to enhance the performance of both people and organizations. Other content providers include Zig Ziglar, Tom Hopkins, and Tony Parinello, to name a few. www.candogo.com

- 2006. Published *The Seven Keys to Effective Business-to-Business Appointment Setting: Unlock Your Sales Potential* (Aspatore Books, 2006).

- 2005. Published *Business-to-Business Prospecting: Innovative Techniques to Get Your Foot in the Door with Any Prospect* (Aspatore Books, 2005).

- March 2005. Named contributing writer for SellingPower.com's *One Minute Tip* featured daily on SellingPower.com.

- 2005–2007. Wrote biweekly column for *The Puget Sound Business Journal* called "Sales Solutions" offering solid sales advice to readers with sales dilemmas.

- Formed a strategic alliance with a local marketing company who purchased rights to sell The Blitz Experience® on CD-ROM.

- Developed The Blitz Experience®, an activity-based sales training program that empowers salespeople to set appointments with qualified prospects the day of the training, resulting in a pipeline full of new opportunities at the end of the day. Trademarked The Blitz Experience® in July 2004.

PARODIVA PRODUCTIONS INC., Redmond, Washington
2002–2003
President and CEO
www.parodivaproductions.com

Founded the company, transforming an idea into a successful corporate entertainment company. Provided clients with customized written song parodies that were performed at corporate events.

- Featured on the front page of the *Seattle Post Intelligencer* business section March 12, 2003 seattlepi.nwsource.com/business/112087_parody12.shtml?sea rchpagefrom=1&searchdiff=684

SASCO, Woodinville, Washington
2001–2002
New Business Development Executive

- Negotiated an additional $25,000 salary than was originally budgeted for the position.
- By introducing a brand new sales methodology to the company, contributed to the successful acquisition of a $7.5MM contract on a local highly visible marquis project.

ACS DATALINE, Bothell, Washington

1999–2001
Regional Sales Manager, Washington and Oregon

- Hired and managed a team of eight Sales Executives in Washington and Oregon.
- Secured 111% of company revenue goal, earning a place in the President's Club.
- Developed a new line of business that brought an additional 20% revenue per year, and added seven new employees to support the new line of business.

LUCENT TECHNOLOGIES INC., Seattle, Washington
1997–1999
Account Executive
- Negotiated signing bonus.

- Recruited from previous position at ChemSearch, successfully negotiated a signing bonus to join the Lucent Technologies sales team.

- Developed new business for Lucent Technologies selling business telephone systems to small and medium-sized businesses.

- Partnered with a Senior Account Executive to sell a business telephone system worth over $250,000.

CHEMSEARCH, Seattle, Washington
1996–1997
Sales Representative

- Managed the South Seattle territory. Sold industrial chemicals to manufacturing companies, trucking companies, and the like. Consistently exceeded revenue goals, earning the prestigious Premier Award.

VOICE-TEL OF WASHINGTON, Bellevue, Washington
1991–1996
Account Executive

- Successfully sold voice-messaging technology when it was brand new to the market place.
- Consistently earned Business Development Achievement Award as a top salesperson in the company.
- Opened the Anchorage, Alaska, office.
- Designed a reseller program just before the company was sold to Premier Technologies.

EDUCATION

BACHELOR OF ARTS IN PSYCHOLOGY
1991
Southwest Texas State University
San Marcos, Texas

EXCELLENT REFERENCES AVAILABLE UPON REQUEST

3

Developing Persuasive Case Studies

Have you had happy employers? You know, the ones who thought you were the greatest and always praised your work? Why not leverage the relationships with those former employers to gain employment now? Detailed accounts of your most successful projects for former employers are your best selling tool. When others have something positive to say about you and the work you did, it establishes credibility with potential employers who are considering hiring you. The case studies you write should be results-oriented so they address what employers care about most when considering job applicants: results. Here I will give examples of two different types of case studies. The first is an example of a summarized case study that is short and to the point, stating facts without much narrative description. The second is an example of a benefits-based, narrative-in-description case study.

Writing a Summarized Case Study

Here is the outline to follow for a summarized case study:

Employer:	Name the former employer for this case study.
Challenge:	State the challenge that faced your employer before or during the time you worked for them.
Solution:	Describe the solution you provided.
Result:	Describe the result based on the solution you provided.

Testimonial: Include a quote from the employer describing the
result you provided for the company.

Here is an example of a summarized case study I have used as a selling
tool for The Blitz Experience sales training program, which started out
as a project I did for a former employer, and which I have since turned
into a full-time business:

Client: ABC Telecommunications Company
Challenge: Revenue was down with the company at 23% of its
line goal.* Sales reps were unmotivated and lacked the
consistency of the activity necessary for the company
to reach its revenue goals.
Solution: The Blitz Experience program including 3 sessions,
45 days apart
Result: 91 appointments with new prospects, 35 new
accounts, and 105% of line goal*

Testimonial: *"Since our Sittig Incorporated Blitz Experience kick-off, our
sales reps have changed their behavior to consistent, proactive
selling activities that have resulted in tremendous revenue growth
for our company. Thanks Sittig Incorporated, we couldn't have
done it without you!"*
- VP Sales, ABC Telecommunications Company

(*Line goal is defined as the number of telephone lines sold with ABC
Telecommunications Company services attached, such as long
distance, local service, DSL, and the like.)

Writing a Benefits-Based Case Study

The second type of case study is called the *Benefits-based, Narrative-
in-description Case Study.* Here is an outline to follow for this type of
case study:

State a description of the former employer in terms of their industry, size, core competency, and/or business purpose or mission.

Employer: Name the former employer for this case study.

Challenge: State the challenge in detail that faced your employer before or during the time you worked for them, focusing on the business pain they were experiencing.

Solution: Describe the solution of the project you provided, focusing on the *benefits* of your solution versus any features associated with your solution.

Result: Describe the result based on the solution you provided, focusing again on the *benefits* of the result.

Testimonial: Include a quote from the former employer describing the result you provided.

Following is an example of this type of case study that I wrote *as a customer* of an audio and Web-based conferencing company I will refer to as XYZ Conference Service.

> Sittig Incorporated is a results-oriented, activity-based sales training and new business development firm that helps companies increase sales through the creation and implementation of effective Blitz Experience, Team Building, and Lead Generation Programs.

> **Challenge:**   Traditional means of presenting to prospects face to face in other states and countries was becoming so expensive and inefficient that I was considering limiting my prospecting efforts to my local area. I needed a solution that would allow me to fully present my sales training programs through both a visual and an audio process in an effort to fully engage

my prospects. I was concerned about the ease of use of a high-tech solution for both my prospects as the participants and myself as the presenter. I was also concerned my prospects might find a Web-based method of presenting my sales training solutions as being unfriendly or impersonal.

Solution: XYZ Conference Service offered not only a user-friendly audio and Web-based visual conferencing solution for Sittig Incorporated and my prospects, but stayed hands-on with me as the conference call facilitator until I was completely comfortable using the service. XYZ's responsiveness to my questions was immediate, and their willingness to help me with trial runs the day before a conference call was incredibly helpful.

Result: Sittig Incorporated has become much more efficient both in the time and expenses associated with presenting sales training programs to prospects in other states and countries, and as a result, I have closed more business! The XYZ Web-based conference solution has been very well received by prospects, as it is both easy to use and offers them the convenience of participating in the conference call from their own home or office. Sittig Incorporated is no longer limited to prospecting in my local area. Because of the XYZ solution, I no longer have boundaries and can literally prospect all over the world!

Testimonial: *"XYZ Conference Service has provided Sittig Incorporated with an invaluable tool that allows unlimited prospecting capabilities. As a result, I have increased my business and my bottom line! I experienced an instant return on investment by using XYZ to develop new business with companies outside my local area."*

- Andrea Sittig-Rolf, President and CEO, Sittig Incorporated

Don't be afraid to ask for testimonials from former employers. When you've done a good job working for a company, ask for their permission to either include them as a case study in your Accomplishments Portfolio, or to give a testimonial regarding the work you've done. Often, former employers are more agreeable if you make it as easy for them as possible.

For example, you should be the one to write the case study or testimonial and just ask your former employer to give you their permission to use it. Not only does this save your former employer time, but it allows you to convey the message you want to convey and to best showcase the work you've done for that particular employer. It also guarantees a faster turnaround of the case study since you're not waiting on your former employer to finish it.

Case studies are also wonderful for overcoming objections. For example, when scheduling job interviews and you hear the objection "I'm not interested," you can refer to a case study of a former employer with a similar objection who had since hired you with great results.

It is a good idea to categorize case studies by industry, company size, and application of your former work. When prospecting for a new job, you can then refer to the case study that best fits the potential employer you are working with. For example, if you are seeking work with a small telecommunications company that will hire you to make their billing process more efficient, share with them a case study that profiles a small telecommunications company that hired you to make their billing process more efficient. This becomes extremely valuable to your potential employer by giving them confidence that you can produce the results they desire.

Case studies should be used throughout the job interview process, from introducing yourself to including them in your Accomplishments Portfolio, overcoming objections, and finally asking for the job. Because case studies highlight the *results* you have been able to create for former employers, they keep your results top of mind with your potential employers. I can almost guarantee that your competitors are not doing this, so all other things being equal, you will gain the competitive advantage by providing for your potential employers what your competitors do not!

Finally, a huge benefit of writing case studies is that in the process, you might identify a project you did or program you created for a former employer that could actually be a business in and of itself. I write about this from personal experience. I used to run sales blitz days for a former employer and was recognized for creating increased revenue and profits for my region. When my boss called to ask me what I was doing to create such fantastic results, I told him that I had been doing blitz days with my sales team to fill the pipeline with new opportunities and start the sales process. He was impressed and told me to "keep up the good work." After having that conversation with him I thought, why would I keep up the good work for him, when I could do it for myself?" That's when The Blitz Experience was born. I soon quit my job and then packaged The Blitz Experience as a program to sell to other companies to help them grow their pipelines with new opportunities. Since 2002, my company has thrived and continues to grow year over year; all because I took an idea that was a program I created for an employer, and turned it into a business.

So, as you're writing your case studies and identifying the different projects and programs you created or were involved in with various employers, think about which ones you enjoyed the most and allowed you to be noticed by your boss. Consider that maybe the right track for you is to start your own business based on what you've done in your past work life.

They say "do what you love and you'll never work a day in your life", and I'm fortunate to be able to say, that's exactly how I feel about what I do. I actually look forward to Mondays!

4

Scheduling Job Interviews

It occurred to me that much of what I teach in my sales training program, The Blitz Experience, when it comes to setting sales appointments, applies to scheduling interviews with prospective employers as well, especially if your approach is to pursue companies that aren't necessarily hiring, but that you think you'd be a perfect match for in the "dream job" you've created based on your Ideal Job Profile. Keep in mind, when applying for an existing job where the prospective employer has an actual job requisition in place, you may not run into "objections" when scheduling interviews. But if you're proposing a *new* job that's not currently being sought by the prospective employer, you'll have more push-back since the prospective employer doesn't yet know they need you. It's your job to effectively schedule the interview so you can propose the job you're seeking and sell yourself as the right person for the job you've created!

Anticipate the objection, **H**andle the objection, **A**sk for the interview. The "Aha!" Formula works every time for securing qualified interviews with decision-makers. It sounds simple, and it is. But so often we're intimidated by the word "no," so rather than handle the objection or perceived rejection, we simply thank the prospective employer, hang up the phone, and make the next call. Imagine, though, having to make fewer job interview phone calls because you have improved your appointment-setting skill level.

Before we get to the heart of this chapter, first we must consider getting past the gatekeeper so that once we have the decision-maker on the phone, we can use the "Aha!" Formula and the overcoming common objections techniques I describe. Here are some examples of how the conversation with the gatekeeper might sound in my business:

> **Receptionist:** "ABC Company, how can I direct your call?"
> **Andrea:** "Hi. My name is Andrea Sittig-Rolf, and I'm with Sittig Incorporated. I'd like to talk to your sales manager, please."
> **Receptionist:** "Can I tell him what this is regarding?"
> **Andrea:** "Sure. We are the developer and exclusive provider of a sales training program called The Blitz Experience, and I'd like to set up a time to meet with him to determine whether this program will be of benefit to ABC Company."
> **Receptionist:** "Is he expecting your call?"
> **Andrea:** "Well, no, not exactly."
> **Receptionist:** "Hold, please."
> **Sales Manager's Voicemail:** "Hi. I can't take your call right now, so please leave a message and I'll call you back as soon as possible."

Sound familiar? Ever get the feeling the receptionist has been trained just to screen your calls and keep you away from connecting with the decision-maker at her company? Well, guess what, she has!

Conversations like the above haunted me in the early years of my sales career. After dealing with this same conversation over and over again, I decided there must be a better way, so I started to experiment. Here's what I learned…

The receptionist can either make or break you in any organization. She holds the key to your success in terms of actually directing you to the person you want to talk to. I've said "her company" and "her organization" previously because as far as you are concerned, it is **her** company. (Or his company, if you're dealing with a male receptionist.) The point is that knowing this, there are a few things you can do.

First, engage the receptionist. Then, be genuine in your approach. Receptionists can smell a rat from hundreds of miles away. That's part of their training, too.

Many times, just by logging on to a company Web site, you can find the name of the chief executive officer or president of the company. Make note of this before making your call. Let's say the chief executive officer of the company you're calling is John Jones. Now, let's take a look at how the conversation with the receptionist should go:

> **Receptionist:** "ABC Company, how can I direct your call?"
>
> **Andrea:** "Hi. My name is Andrea Sittig-Rolf, and I'm with Sittig Incorporated. I'm hoping you can help me. I'm looking for the person in your organization who would make a decision regarding sales training. That wouldn't be John Jones, would it?"
>
> **Receptionist:** "Oh no, that wouldn't be John Jones. That would be Bob Smith."
>
> **Andrea:** "Great! Can I speak to Bob, please?"
>
> **Receptionist:** "Sure, I'll transfer you."
>
> **Andrea:** "Thank you."

Believe it or not, most of the time, this technique works and will get you to the person you need to talk to. The idea is that the receptionist doesn't want to bother John Jones, the chief executive officer, with a cold call from someone looking for a job. It's almost a relief for her to be able to transfer you to Bob Smith, someone below John Jones on the organizational chart at the company.

Even if you are unable to speak to Bob Smith during this particular phone call, at least now you have the name of the person you need to talk to for the next time you call. Receptionists don't screen calls as much when you have the name of the person you want to talk to.

Another technique that works well is to ask for the "help desk." You will not get screened when asking for the help desk, and the people there are more likely to transfer your call to the appropriate person.
On another note, I know it seems obvious, but for goodness sake, say "please" and "thank you." You would not believe the salespeople I've trained who don't even say "please" and "thank you" when dealing with receptionists, or anyone else for that matter. Simple courtesy goes a long way, especially when looking for a job.

In the situation where you are talking to someone other than the receptionist who you realize is not the decision-maker and they tell you, "I'm not the one to talk to," do not say, "Oh, well who is?" Instead say, "Really? What is it you do?" and again, engage the person in conversation for a bit before asking who you should talk to instead. The person you're talking to will be much more likely to help direct your call to the right person if you engage them in conversation and take an interest in them first.

Another tip is to avoid dealing with the gatekeeper at all and simply ask for the sales department immediately when the receptionist answers. Believe me, callers are not screened when calling on the sales department, for obvious reasons. Then, when you get a salesperson on the phone, say something like, "Hi. I'm not sure if you can help me, but I'm actually hoping to talk to [title of person you're looking for]. Who would that be?" Salespeople are not trained to screen calls and they love to talk, so chances are you'll get plenty of information about the company you're calling on as well as the person you ultimately need to talk to. You can also ask for human resources, another department that is likely to help direct your call to the appropriate person.

Finally, when the receptionist answers, you can also try asking for the accounting or accounts receivable department. You won't get screened by the receptionist from those departments either, and people in those departments aren't trained to screen calls, so chances are, they'll give you the information you need.

Okay, now that you're past the gatekeeper and you have the chance to actually speak to the decision-maker, let's briefly look at your opening script when calling on a new prospective employer for the first time. The purpose of your phone call is to *get the interview*. Therefore, you should say so right up front. Also, the point of meeting with the prospective employer is not just to tell them about how great you are, but rather to learn about them and their company to better understand what solution you can provide. You should address this in your opening script, and it should go something like this:

> "Hi, Mr. Prospective Employer. My name is Andrea Sittig Rolf, and I have extensive experience in helping companies [results you've created for former employers]. The reason for my call today is to schedule an interview to learn more about your organization so we can determine whether there is a fit for me within your firm. How's Thursday at 10:15 a.m. work for you?"

Your opening script should include a brief overview of who you are and what you do, and then get right to the point of scheduling the interview. The reason for your call is to get the interview, not to sell what you can do. Avoid the temptation to answer a myriad of questions. Sometimes, prospective employers will engage you over the phone in an effort to avoid meeting with you in person, and by engaging in a long, drawn-out conversation, you may talk yourself right out of the interview. Instead, stay focused and remember that your extended conversation should happen in person and not over the phone. Also, remember that the purpose of your interview is to both tell them about your experience and results you've created for past employers, and to learn more about them, and it is important to convey this message during your opening script (i.e., "The reason for my call today is to schedule an interview to learn more about your organization so we can determine whether there is a fit for me within your firm. How's Thursday at 10:15 a.m. work for you?").

Before you can begin to share all of your wonderful benefits, you must first learn about your prospective employer to determine whether there is a fit between them and you. More about this will be covered later, but for now, I will explain how to overcome the most common objections and get the interview by using the proven methodology of the "Aha!" Formula.

Okay, now that you're past the gatekeeper and you have had a chance to try your opening script with the prospect, here is when the "Aha!" Formula kicks in. Now, you may be saying to yourself, "Yeah, I get it. The 'Aha!' Formula makes sense, but how do I overcome the objection? What exactly do I say in response to the objection, and how do I handle it and then get the interview anyway?" I'm so glad you asked!

As good as your opening script is, most of the time you will encounter objections from your prospective employer while scheduling the interview. After years of conducting The Blitz Experience, as well as taking some good advice from Stephan Schiffman, author of a fantastic book on cold calling called *Cold Calling Techniques...That Really Work!* (5th edition, Adams Media, 2003), the most common objections you will hear fall into the nine categories below:

1. "We're all set."
2. "I'm not interested."
3. "I'm too busy."
4. "Send me your résumé."
5. "We don't have money to hire anyone right now."
6. "What makes you so good?" or "Why should I consider hiring you?"
7. "Just give me the thirty-second version of your pitch."
8. "We're not in the market to hire anyone right now."
9. "How much are you asking?"

As I mentioned in the "Aha!" Formula, the key is to anticipate and handle the objection properly before asking for the interview, and always ask for the interview after handling the objection. Keep in mind that you may hear more than one objection in any given phone call. In other words, the prospect may say, "I'm not interested," and after handling that objection you might hear, "We're all set," and then you might hear, "We don't have any money to hire anyone right now." Prospective employers may give multiple objections, some of them true, some of them false and just used as a tool to get you off the phone. While it's important not to take the first "No" for an answer, I don't recommend overcoming more than three objections in any given phone call. Sometimes, the answer is "No." However, by learning how to overcome the most common objections, you'll significantly increase your interviews ratio. In this chapter, I will give many examples of exactly how to overcome each of the most common objections you will hear when making phone calls to schedule interviews with prospective employers.

"We're all set." Also known as "status quo," this is probably the most difficult objection to overcome, because people don't want to change unless there is a compelling reason to do so. The key to handling this particular objection is to describe how you *complement, enhance, or supplement* what the prospective employer is already doing. In other words, don't put yourself in the position of competing with the prospect's current person in a similar role, and possibly insulting the prospect's earlier decision to go with that other person. Instead, you will actually enhance what that current person is already doing. This works so well because now the prospective employer doesn't have to choose one or the other, but can instead have both: the former decision they made regarding the person doing something similar to what you're proposing can simply be enhanced by what you can provide. By using this technique, you're actually reinforcing what the prospect is already doing by showing that you will fit into their particular plan.

To understand the practicality of this technique, the example below demonstrates exactly how this technique can be used:

> **You:** "Hi, Mr. Prospective Employer. My name is
> _____ and I'm an expert in [results you've created
> for a former employer]. The reason for my call today
> is to schedule an interview to learn more about your
> organization so we can determine whether there is a
> fit for me within your firm. How's Thursday at 10:15
> a.m. work for you?"
> **Prospective Employer:** (Anticipate the objection.)
> "We're all set with folks who have a similar role at
> our company."
> **You:** "That's great! May I ask what some of the tasks
> and duties are associated with that role and what
> benefits have been created for your company as a
> result?"
> **Prospective Employer:** "Sure, [their explanation]."
> **You:** (Handle the objection.) "Well, that's perfect
> actually, because I can enhance what that person is
> doing by [how you can enhance what they're doing]."
> (Ask for the interview.) "Why don't I come by next
> Thursday at 10:15a.m. to learn more about your

company so we can determine whether I might be a
fit for your firm?"
Prospective Employer: "Okay."

(Now I realize at first glance, this may seem a bit of a stretch; but the
point it, you just want to GET THE INTERVIEW. Once you are
meeting with the decision maker face-to-face, you'll have the
opportunity to learn more about their organization and about what
other opportunities might be available to you, even if the original idea
you had is not an option. The idea is that if you don't at least get the
interview, you won't have the opportunity to learn about what else
might be going on at that organization that might actually be a good fit
for you.)

Notice the "Aha!" Formula used throughout the script. By anticipating
the objection, I was ready to handle the objection and then ask for the
interview. Easy, right? It's actually not too bad when all you have to do
is overcome one objection and then get the interview. However, as I
mentioned previously, sometimes prospects will give more than one
objection. Using the same example above, the multiple objections
script might go something like this:

> **You:** "Hi, Mr. Prospective Employer. My name is
> _____ and I'm an expert in [results you've created
> for a former employer]. The reason for my call today
> is to schedule an interview to learn more about your
> organization so we can determine whether there is a
> fit for me within your firm. How's Thursday at 10:15
> a.m. work for you?"
> **Prospective Employer:** (**A**nticipate the objection.)
> "We're all set with folks who have a similar role at
> our company."
> **You:** "That's great! May I ask what some of the tasks
> and duties are associated with that role and what

benefits have been created for your company as a
result?"

Prospective Employer: "Sure, [their explanation]."

You: (**H**andle the objection.) "Well, that's perfect
actually, because I can enhance what that person is
doing by [how you can enhance what they're doing]."
(**A**sk for the interview.) "Why don't I come by next
Thursday at 10:15 a.m. to learn more about your
company so we can determine whether I might be a
fit for your firm?"

Prospect: (**A**nticipate the objection.) "Why don't you
just send me your résumé?"

You: (**H**andle the objection.) "I'd be happy to send
you my résumé, and I have found it to be more useful
when having the opportunity to review in person."
(**A**sk for the interview.) "Why don't I just come by
Thursday at 10:15 a.m. to learn more about your
organization, and I'll bring my résumé with me?"

Prospective Employer: "Okay."

In this scenario, if the prospective employer had given me one more
objection, I would handle it and ask for the interview for the last time.
Beyond overcoming three objections in a row, your prospecting phone
call turns into an argument, which is the last impression you want to
leave with the prospective employer when hanging up the phone!
After hearing three objections, simply thank the prospective employer,
hang up, and make your next call.

Let's move on to the next category, "I'm not interested," probably
heard more often than any other objection when prospecting for job
interviews with companies who may not be hiring. The key here is to
describe the *result* you can provide and, more specifically, the result
you've provided for someone else (i.e., another employer). Here's what
to say when you have **A**nticipated the objection and the prospective
employer tells you they're not interested:

You: (Handle the objection.) "You know, Mr. Prospective Employer, that's what a couple of my former employers said before they understood that by hiring me they would [result former employers have experienced by hiring you]." (**A**sk for the interview.) "Why don't I just come by at 10:15 a.m. next Thursday so I can share with you some actual results other employers have had as a result of hiring me?"

Notice here you explain a typical result previous employers have had from working with you: "You know, Mr. Prospective Employer, that's what many of my previous employers said before they understood that I could [result you've created for a former employer]." By immediately explaining a compelling result, you are more likely to get the interview.

Next, the "I'm too busy" objection is also quite common. The beauty of this objection is that you don't want to talk to them now anyway; you want to schedule an interview to talk in person! If they're too busy to talk, that's the very reason to set an appointment, so you can talk face to face when they're less busy and have scheduled you in their calendar. Another technique that works well here is if they're too busy to talk and they ask you to call back to schedule the interview, suggest that you *tentatively* schedule an interview now and that you'll call back to confirm. Microsoft conducted a study that showed there is a 70 percent greater chance an activity will happen if it's scheduled in the calendar. So, in our scenario, there is a 70 percent greater likelihood the prospective employer will honor the interview with you if you can get him or her to put it in their calendar. With multiple objections given on this particular call, it might go something like this:

Prospective Employer: (Anticipate the objection.) "You've caught me at a time when I'm too busy to talk."

You: (Handle the objection, Ask for the interview.) "Okay, well then rather than taking time now, why don't I just come by next Thursday at 10:15 a.m.?"

Prospective Employer: (Anticipate the objection.) "Well, why don't you call me back to schedule the interview?"

You: (Handle the objection, Ask for the interview.) "I'd be happy to, but why don't we go ahead and tentatively get it on the calendar now, and I'll call back to confirm?"

Prospective Employer: "Okay, what did you say? Next Thursday at 10:15 a.m.? See you then."

Even with up to three objections in one call, each should be Anticipated and Handled, and you should always Ask for the interview. This is the "Aha!" Formula in action. It's probably a more aggressive approach than you're used to, but in this economic climate, it may take a lot more effort on your part to land job interviews and lock out your competitors than what you've had to do in the past.

The next popular category of objection is "Send me your résumé." I actually quite enjoy this objection, because I have a funny way to handle it. Feel free to use this one for those of you who are brave enough to do so! When the prospect has told me, "Send me your résumé," or more often in my job as a salesperson and entrepreneur, "Send me some literature," I have Anticipated this objection and here's how I Handle it: "I'd be happy to send you some literature, but just so you know the package it comes in is five feet eight inches, 150 pounds, with dark hair (Ask for the interview), and it'll be there Thursday at 10:15 a.m.!" Obviously, the package I'm describing is myself and not an actual package, but it gets a laugh every time and gets the interview or sales appointment most of the time! The point is to use humor when you can. Most people will appreciate it, and it will break the ice and give you leverage to actually getting the interview.

Another common objection you might hear is, "We don't have money to hire anyone now" or "It's just not in the budget." During one of my Blitz Experience role-play exercises, I used the objection "I don't have any money" with the salesperson. I loved his response. He said to me, "Well, neither do I. That's why I'm calling you!" He said he actually uses this technique and it works most of the time because he gets the prospect to laugh, thus letting his guard down, allowing the salesperson to get the appointment. Again, humor can be an effective technique when scheduling job interviews too!

A more serious way to handle this objection might sound like this:

> **Prospective Employer:** (Anticipate the objection.) "It's not in our budget right now."
> **You:** (Handle the objection.) "In that case, now is the perfect time to meet, before you're even in the market for a position like this so I can take my time to learn more about your organization and I might be of benefit somewhere down the road." (Ask for the interview.) "Why don't I just come by at 10:15 a.m. on Thursday so I can learn more about your firm and share more about how I might [result you've created for a past employer]?"
> **Prospective Employer:** "Okay, see you then."

Another situation you may run into with prospects is having them ask you, "What makes you so good?" or "Why should I consider hiring you?" This is the prospect employer's way of getting you to give your entire pitch over the phone, making the interview unnecessary. Don't get caught up in this scenario. Instead, it should go something like this.

> **Prospective Employer:** (Anticipate the objection.) "What makes you so good?"

You: (Handle the objection.) "Lots of things! That's the very reason we should meet!" (Ask for the interview.) "How's Thursday at 10:15 a.m.?"

Another trick prospective employers often use goes like this:

Prospective Employer: (Anticipate the objection.) "Just give me the thirty-second version of your pitch."
You: (Handle the objection.) "I would be doing a great disservice to both of us to try and do that, which is exactly why we should get together." (Ask for the interview.) "How's Friday at noon for lunch?"

Another common objection you may hear is "We're not in the market right now." Here's how this should go:

Prospective Employer: (Anticipate the objection.) "We're not in the market to hire anyone right now."
You: (Handle the objection.) "Great, because now is actually the best time to meet, before you're in the market, so you can take your time to learn about what I have to offer to your company so then when you are hiring, we've already had the initial conversation." (Ask for the interview.) "How's Thursday at 10:15 a.m.?"

Finally, another objection that sounds like a hiring signal goes like this:

Prospective Employer: (Anticipate the objection.) "How much are you asking?"
You: (Handle the objection.) "Well that depends on several factors, and I'd be doing both of us a disservice to try and give you a dollar amount over the phone." (Ask for the interview.) "Why don't we

just get together Thursday at 10:15 a.m. so I can learn more about your company and share some of the results I've created for other employers to determine the appropriate salary?"

When all else fails and you can't remember how to handle which objection, remember one technique I call "the conversation technique." I am blown away by how well this particular technique works. The key here is to handle the objection by asking an open-ended question (i.e., a question beginning with "Who," "What," "Why," "Where," "When," "How," or statements such as "Please describe," "Tell me about," or "Help me understand"). What this does is engage the prospective employer in conversation. Once they are engaged, say, "You know, it sounds like we have a lot to talk about. Why don't I come by next Thursday at 10:15 a.m. to learn more about your business and determine how we might work together?"

In practicing this technique, something that commonly happens is the prospective employer will begin to ask you questions. The temptation for most people is to answer all of their questions right then. After all, they must be interested if they're asking so many questions, right? Actually, what can happen is that you've answered all the questions that need to be answered and had an entire conversation about you, so there's no need to schedule the interview! You have literally talked yourself out of the interview. Instead, the conversation technique teaches you to leverage the fact that you're having a conversation as the reason to meet in person.

Using the same objection, here's another example using the open-ended phrase "Tell me about," which allows the prospective employer to elaborate on the hot buttons most important to him or her:

> **Prospective Employer:** (Anticipate the objection.)
> "We're not interested in hiring anyone now."

You: (Handle the objection using the open-ended phrase "Tell me about.") "Okay. Will you please tell me about what you're doing now in the area of [describe your expertise]?"

Prospective Employer: [their response].

You: (Handle the objection.) "Yes, that's true of most [role they've describe]. The difference with what I can provide is [what sets you apart from others who do the same job]." (Ask for the interview.) "Why don't I swing by Thursday at 10:15 a.m., and I'll share with you some of the positive, direct results other employers have had?"

Prospective Employer: "Okay."

By engaging the prospective employer in conversation, I now have the perfect reason to meet in person. Remember that the key open-ended questions begin with "Who," "What," "Where," "Why," "When," and "How," and the key open-ended statements or phrases are "Tell me about," "Please describe," or "Help me understand." Engage your prospective employer in conversation over the phone, and use your conversation as the reason to schedule the interview.

The point is that with all of these objections, use the "Aha!" Formula every time to greatly increase your chances of getting the interview and starting the process with new prospective employers.

In addition to learning how to effectively overcome common objections, an equally important lesson here is that you schedule an appointment or appointments with yourself each week to make your interview-scheduling calls. Often, prospecting for new jobs is the activity that gets put on the back burner when it's actually the most important in terms of keeping a full pipeline of prospective employers. Scheduling this time with yourself will predict your close ratio down the road, help you maintain consistency, and create the habits that will guarantee your success at landing your dream job.

A final note about scheduling interviews. You've probably noticed in the scripts so far that I keep asking for interviews on the *quarter* hour (e.g., "Thursday at 10:15 a.m."). There's a reason for this. One is that it makes it easy for your prospective employer to flip to that time on their calendar and if it doesn't work, the question becomes *when* to meet, not *if* you should meet, and *when* to meet is a much better conversation to have. Also, they'll be caught off guard when you ask for a "10:15 a.m." interview rather than on the hour (i.e. "10:00 a.m."). This will set you apart from others calling to schedule interviews and other appointments, and it lets the prospective employer know that you're busy, and that 10:15 a.m. is what works best for you. From there, after you've thrown out the first meeting time as a suggestion, if that doesn't work for the prospective employer, ask what's best for them and go from there to schedule a mutually convenient time to meet. The point is to remain in control of the call, you need to suggest the specific date and time to meet first, then go from there and negotiate a different meeting time if necessary.

In addition to knowing how to schedule interviews once you get the prospective employer on the phone, knowing how to leave effective voicemail messages is equally important. The key to leaving an effective voicemail message is: "Less is more." In other words, the shorter your voicemail message, the better, and the more likely you are to get a response from the prospective employer. The common mistake most of us tend to make is that we consider voicemail an opportunity to leave a three-minute commercial, rather than the more appropriate use of voicemail, to get the prospective employer to call us back.

Many times, we leave voicemail messages that are so detailed that the prospective employers decide they are not interested and do not call us back. The better tactic is to leave a short, concise message that includes an element of curiosity so the prospective employer is intrigued and therefore has a reason to return the call.

For example, referring to a well-known company in the prospective employer's industry for whom you have worked creates curiosity. Using this technique, your voicemail message might sound something like this:

> "Hi, Mr. Prospective Employer. This is [your name]. I'm calling about [ABC Company]. Will you please return my call at [your phone number]? Thank you."

That's it, nothing more, hang up. Now, the strategy to this technique working successfully is in the way you handle the conversation when the prospective employer calls you back. To avoid the prospective employer feeling tricked into calling you back, here is how the return call should be handled:

> **Prospect:** "Yes, I'm just returning your call about ABC Company."
> **Andrea:** "Great! Thanks for calling me back. ABC Company is a former employer of mine for whom I've worked and [quantify results you have created]. Because you are in a similar industry, I thought we might be able to work together in the same way. Are you available to meet next Thursday at 10:15 a.m. for about thirty minutes to discuss this further?"

By immediately referring back to ABC Company as the reason why you called, you avoid the prospective employer feeling deceived into returning your call, and you are immediately showing the connection between you, and your prospective employer.

Another version of this voicemail that is a little more direct is the following:

> "Hi, Mr. Prospective Employer. This is [your name]. I'm calling to tell you about some of the fantastic

results I've created for companies such as [other companies for whom you've worked]. Will you please return my call at [your phone number]? Thank you."

Speaking to the results you've created for other companies gives you credibility, and being brief in the voicemail message you leave creates curiosity, both of which will increase your chances of getting a return phone call.

One final technique that works well after you've already had your first interview with the prospective employer goes something like this, should you need to leave a voicemail message:

> "Hi, Mr. Prospective Employer. This is [your name]. I have just a few more questions for you. Will you please return my call at your earliest convenience? I can be reached at [your phone number]. Thank you."

The idea here is to let the prospective employer know you have more questions. This is much more effective than the traditional voicemail message we might leave for a prospective employer after an interview, which might go something like this:

> "Hi, Mr. Prospective Employer. This is [your name]. I just wanted to give you a quick call to follow up on our meeting. Please feel free to give me a call if you have any questions. I can be reached at [your phone number]. Thank you."

Do you see the difference? In the first example, I've suggested asking the prospective employer to call you back because you have more questions. In the second example, I suggest asking the prospective employer to call you if he had any questions. The reason the first example is so much more effective is that it implies there are some loose ends that need to be dealt with, whereas the second example asks the prospective employer to call back only if he has questions. If he doesn't have questions, and he most likely won't, there's no reason for him to call you back.

In addition to leveraging voicemail as a powerful tool when leaving messages for prospects, it can also be a powerful tool when leaving a greeting, also known as the outgoing message, on your own voicemail. While attending a client sales conference several years ago, I had the privilege of participating in a workshop facilitated by Shawna Schuh entitled "Power Tools to Build Your Business." During the workshop, she explained how to use voicemail as a "power tool" when recording your outgoing greeting by using the acronym VOICE, as follows:

V = Visual
Let your voice convey a feeling, some emotion so the caller pictures you in a positive way.
O = Optimistic
Be up and have a smile in your voice, be happy that someone called.
I = Interesting
Most voicemail messages are boring, mundane, and the same, so making yours different and interesting is a definite advantage.
C = Clever
Let the caller know you appreciate them, want to speak to them, and get them thinking.
E = Energetic
Conveying energy over the phone is the best way to make a positive impression so people will leave a message.

The idea with leaving an effective voicemail greeting or outgoing message is not to give your callers instructions on what to do once they've reached your voicemail. Voicemail has been around long enough now that we all know what to do! We don't have to be told, "I'm either away from my office or on the other line. Please leave a message at the sound of the tone and I'll get back to you as soon as I can." Duh! We know that, right? So by way of example, Shawna suggests the following:

1. "Hi! You've reached the office of Ted Buick. I'm happy you called, and I promise to get back to you today by 5:00."
Note: Only make a promise if you absolutely, positively intend to keep it always.

2. "Hello, this is Julie Mustang with the Road Runner Company. It's a pleasure to serve you, so expect a return call soon."
Note: Be sincere. If you dislike serving people, don't say you like it!

3. "Hi! You've reached the voice of Todd Chevrolet, which is as close to me as you'll come today. I will be returning calls on Thursday if you leave a message. Until then, you can call Julie at extension 202 for immediate service."
Note: There is no mention of where Todd is—no one cares!

4. "It's the voice of Buck Chrysler, and I think it's great that you called. Details are ideal, so leave me some and I'll get back to you soon."
Note: All of these examples were taken from the book *How to Nail Voice Mail* by Shawna Schuh, which you can order online at www.businessgraces.com.

In addition to leveraging voicemail as a powerful interview-scheduling tool, an example of how e-mail is used as a powerful interview-scheduling tool is as follows. Send an e-mail of introduction including something of value to the prospective employer that isn't necessarily selling to them, but rather is providing useful information that will help the prospective employer in their business. For instance, you may know something that's going on in the prospect's industry and could include an article or press release that offers pertinent information and then offer to meet in person to discuss what's going on in their industry.

Some other compelling topics of conversation include strategy discussions, marketplace discussions, and industry trends discussions. In other words, the reason for your meeting in person is to discuss these issues in general, which may be more appealing to your prospective employer. Then, when you're in front of your prospect face to face, you will have the opportunity to discuss the specifics of these topics and how your expertise may be relevant to their business initiatives. (Here's where your Giga Alerts come in handy!)

Better yet, when you are referred to a new prospective employer, put the name of the person who referred you in the subject line of the e-mail. Assuming the person who has referred you is known by the prospect, you can guarantee your e-mail will be opened.

Another technique that works well is to send an e-mail as a follow-up after the initial meeting, and if the prospective employer doesn't respond within a week, send the *exact same e-mail* again one week after sending it the first time. Do not change a thing from your initial e-mail, and do not reference that you've sent it before. The reason this works is that by sending the same e-mail more than once, it acts as a reminder to the prospective employer without insulting them by telling them, "Hey, I've sent this before and you still haven't responded!" You can keep track of the e-mails you send in Microsoft Outlook either in a folder or as a "to do" on your calendar. Send the same initial follow-up e-mail you sent three times, one week apart. Usually by the second or third time you send it, you will get a response.

Also, try alternating leaving voicemail messages and sending e-mail so you give the prospective employer the option of either calling you back or sending an e-mail based on what's most convenient for them.

Now, there is a limit to how often to follow up and for what length of time to continue following up. If the prospective employer is completely unresponsive after you've sent the same e-mail three times and have left several voicemail messages over a period of a month or more, stop following up for now. If prospects ignore you after many attempts on your part, they are either not interested or something has happened in their business or personal life that is preventing them from getting back to you.

Additionally, there are also some things you can do to minimize hearing objections and/or being ignored in the first place. For example, using a creative mailer in advance to get the prospective employer's attention and let him or her know you'll be calling works well to reduce the likelihood of objections when you make your call.

I've practiced several effective strategies over the years that make the interview-scheduling call much easier, and I always get a positive response from prospects.

First, send mail, unfolded, in a nine-by-twelve, brightly colored envelope. Handwrite the name and address of your prospective employer on the envelope. Be sure to include enough postage, as the larger envelopes require more postage than the standard-size envelopes.

Next, handwrite a message on the back flap of the envelope to get their attention, such as, "Referred by [referral source]" or "Information you requested enclosed" or "Information as promised" or "Looking forward to meeting you." Anything you can write on the back flap of the envelope that creates curiosity will inspire the prospective employer to actually open and read your materials.

Mail something bulky. For example, mail one baby shoe with your business card attached and write a note on the back of your card that says, "Just wanted to get my foot in the door," or something else that relates to your expertise. (Oh, and if you haven't already had business cards made with your name, contact information, and expertise as well as a testimonial from a former employer on the back, do it immediately. Looking for a job *is* your job now, so you should have a business card to distribute in mailers as well as at networking events, interviews, job fairs, and the like.)

Okay, back to the mailer. For example, I often mail a party horn to prospects. One, it's a prop I use in my sales training programs, so it's directly relevant to my business. Two, it's bulky so it creates curiosity. And three, it immediately sends a message that my program is *fun*, an important part of my brand that is easily conveyed using this technique. Be sure to include a return address on the outside of the envelope so it's sure to be delivered by the post office.

Get the prospective employer's attention by sending the "skeleton mailer," to be used only as a last resort! I learned this one from Jerry Hocutt. When a prospective employer you have been trying to reach has not responded to your many voice messages, send a rubber skeleton in a nine-by-twelve, brightly colored envelope. Attach a business card to the toe of the skeleton by punching a hole in the business card and tying it on the skeleton's toe with a short ribbon. On the back of the business card, write, "This is me, waiting for you, to call me back." Most people who have a sense of humor will respond to this, although you must choose carefully which prospects to send it to, based on the rapport you have with the prospective employer.

The last strategy to get a response is to mail items that are tactile in nature, in other words, something to feel and interact with, again using something that relates to your expertise. Again, the party horn in my business works great, so think about something tactile that relates to your expertise that you could mail.

5

Empowering Others to Promote You

What is an ambassador? An ambassador is the best advocate you'll ever have, and the fastest way to bring you to prospective employers. Having an ambassador is like having a recruiter who works just for you. Specifically, an ambassador is someone who is a friend, colleague, associate, or former employer or who believes wholeheartedly in you and what you can deliver to a prospective employer's organization. So much so, that as your ambassador they are willing to *promote* you among their peers and colleagues, as well as within their own organization and other organizations that might be hiring. Winning ambassadors requires that you can demonstrate the following three criteria.

First, it's not enough anymore to simply *save* an employer time and money. You must now be able to show that what you offer will actually *make* your employer money, actually increase their revenue, and improve their bottom line. Keep in mind that there are creative ways of showing this if what you do can't be shown in hard dollars but will improve your employer's bottom line. For example, if you have formerly worked for a printing company, it's pretty tough to show that printing business cards, brochures, and other marketing collateral will make money for an employer. But what if the quality of work you do is so much better than that of your employer's competition that you can show your print job will get noticed, more than that of your employer's competition? What if your print job presents a better image for your employer than the competition's print job? What if you are able to make recommendations to your employer, based on their specific requirements, as to the appropriate paper, ink, formatting, etc., so that the marketing collateral you print for them is exactly the image they want to portray? Then couldn't you argue that by allowing your employer to present a better image up front, based on the quality of work you provide, your employer is more likely to get that extra deal or two a year? What is an extra deal or two a year worth, in terms of hard dollars, to your employer?

The reason I use this as an example is because I was a client of a local printing company that, I found out later, did *not* make the right recommendations to me in terms of ink, paper, and formatting. As such, I found out about a year later that the brochure I had been sending in the mail was completely smeared with ink and actually looked dirty by the time my prospect received it! It was only when I was considering using a new printing company for a new brochure that I discovered this. The new printer asked to see copies of my old brochure so he would have a feel for the type of paper, ink, etc. my project would require, so I mailed him an old brochure. When we met in person to go over my options for the new brochure, he showed me the old brochure I had sent him in the mail. I was horrified to think I'd been sending that brochure in the mail for the past year to so many prospects! The inside of the brochure was black and red ink printed on glossy white paper. Because of the paper and ink combination my previous printer used, the black and red ink had smeared all over the white glossy paper. The ink was dry, but due to the movement of the brochure pages against each other within the envelope, the ink had created smudges all over the inside of the brochure. Needless to say, I never used my previous printing company again. The new printing company I began working with won my current and all of my future business based on his recommendations of how to improve the smeared ink problem by using a heavier, better-quality paper and a different type of ink that would not smear. Now I actually receive compliments on my new brochures not only for the design, but for the quality of the paper and crispness of the ink. I'm convinced that I will earn that extra deal or two a year based on the first impression I am now presenting when I send out a new brochure as my first point of contact with a new prospect. An extra deal or two a year could be worth tens of thousands of dollars to me, so I conclude that by using this new printing company, I am actually making more money now than I was when I used my old printing company!

The second ambassador-winning criterion is that you need to make your ambassador look good to their peers. In other words, the ambassador needs to feel proud that they discovered you, like you are a golden nugget or a little-known treasure that only your ambassador found. Meeting this criterion requires that you provide the very best work possible to your employer. You must under-promise and over-deliver in every case when dealing with your ambassador and their peers. From meeting your ambassador's colleagues for the first time, to eventually landing the job, you must consistently provide the best-quality work available anywhere in your industry. Finally, if your ambassador prefers it, keep them apprised of your dealings with those they are promoting you to. Your ambassador may or may not want you to do this, so just ask and they will let you know.

I have several ambassadors who consistently promote my Blitz Experience program to their peers, colleagues, and channel partners. One of them is a marketing firm that actually builds my program into the marketing plans she provides for her clients. Another ambassador, who is the president of a commercial furniture manufacturing rep firm, asked me to create a PowerPoint presentation for him to present to his industry manufacturing companies and dealer network in an effort to sell my programs! Finally, my most well-known ambassador, a software manufacturing company, promotes my programs to their original equipment manufacturers network. Without exception, I've shown each of my ambassadors how my offering will make them money and make them look good. I also keep them apprised of my dealings with those they have recommended to me. Now that this ambassador network has been established, it continues to grow exponentially and I find myself doing less marketing and more delivering of my programs, resulting in the hiring of several new employees to meet the demand my ambassador network has created. My company has become more profitable because I am spending less time and energy marketing my programs and looking for new clients and more time doing the work I get paid for, which is implementing my programs!

Ambassadors are the cheapest recruiting team you will ever find. You don't have to pay them a salary. You don't even have to pay them a commission or bonus and you don't have to offer any extravagant incentives, although it is nice to appreciate your ambassadors as much as you can by taking them to lunch every now and then and remembering them during the holidays! This model of searching for a job is extremely effective and valuable when you consider the time and money you will save in finding a new employer. Just find a few ambassadors and let them seek and find your prospective new employers for you!

Have you ever wondered how you could leverage a former employer as an ambassador to help you get a new job? Have you considered that if you have, in fact, created outstanding results for your former employer and they're happy with the work you did for them, that they might just be willing to return the favor? Introducing your prospective employers to a former employer creates a compelling environment for your prospective employers to decide to hire you.

To clarify, the difference between this technique of leveraging or empowering ambassadors to *get a new job* versus empowering ambassadors to *promote* you is that when you leverage them to *get a new job*, **you** are the one bringing the prospective employer and former employer together to have a discussion about the work you provided and the outstanding results you created. When empowering ambassadors to *promote* your business, the ambassadors are bringing the prospective employers to you to try to get the job.

Just as an example of how I've used this technique in my own business, one of my clients, a U.S.-based company with a large presence in Canada, provided a great opportunity for leveraging an ambassador relationship to close a deal. After working with this client for about a year in the United States conducting over a dozen sales training days for various locations, I wanted to explore the opportunity to do sales training for them in Canada.

Rather than cold calling the company's Canadian office, I decided to empower Beth, one of my ambassadors who works for my client in the United States, to set up a conference call with the sales managers in Canada. Luckily, she was glad to do it, and after a few conference calls listening to her promote my Blitz Experience program to her Canadian counterparts, I closed the business: five days of training for 130 reps in Canada, my largest single piece of business to date!

So, the next time you are in the predicament of having to find a new job, consider one of your former employers that was happy with the work you did for them. Take into account the type of industry, company size, annual revenue, or other relevant factors that pertain to your prospective employer, and match that prospect up with a former employer that has some or all of the same characteristics.

Once you find common ground between your prospective employer and the former employer, reach out to your former employer and ask if they would be willing to sit down with you and your prospective employer to discuss the work you did for your former employer and how it was beneficial. You will find that most happy former employers are more than willing to do this if you just ask, especially if you were laid off due to the economy, rather than as a result of poor performance.

During the meeting, after making the introductions and explaining to the prospective employer the work you did for your former employer, watch what happens next. As I've illustrated with my own experience using this technique, chances are, your former employer will jump right in and sing your praises to your prospective employer, making landing that dream job a no-brainer.

6

Assembling Accomplishments Portfolio Contents

You may not have all of the things listed in the contents on the template in Appendix A, and that's okay. Just use what you have now and contact former supervisors, managers, customers, colleagues, associates, and professors to help fill in the blanks. You may also have different categories than I show here, and that's okay too. Your gifts and experience will be different than mine, but this should give you a good idea of what kind of information to include in your Accomplishments Portfolio.

Before assembling your Accomplishments Portfolio, read through these tips:

- Purchase a three-ring binder wide enough to just fit the contents of your Accomplishments Portfolio. Make sure it has a clear sleeve on the front cover for you to include a title page with your name and "Accomplishments Portfolio" typed on it.
- Purchase the number of binder/notebook tabs to match the number of categories of your Accomplishments Portfolio.
- Copy the same order of contents for your Accomplishments Portfolio that I have provided in the template in Appendix A. (You may need to add or subtract categories based on your specific needs.)

- The Accomplishments Portfolio cover below goes both on the outside, under the clear sleeve of the three-ring binder, and as the first page of the Accomplishments Portfolio on the inside of the notebook.

- Your standard résumé goes on the inside-left pocket of the three-ring binder (use a paperclip, not a staple, if it's more than one page), as well as on the inside main contents of the binder as item number one. **Note:** Your standard résumé should include a testimonial about you, centered, at the top of the page, as the very first thing on the page.

- The cover letter should be addressed to each potential employer individually, using some of the language you find on their Web site that matches the description of the job you're applying for, if you're applying for an existing job. If you're creating your own dream job, be sure to touch on all of your accomplishments relevant to your dream job in the cover letter. **Note:** Your cover letter should have a different testimonial than the one on your résumé, centered, at the top of the page, as the very first thing on the page.

- Tab 5 in the template, "Case Studies," refers to stories of pain points or problems a former employer had that you solved. Keep this short and to the point using this formula:

  o   Business issue/problem/pain point
  o   Solution you provided
  o   Result of your solution—how it impacted the bottom line of your former employer
  o   Testimonial from former employer about your solution (Write this yourself and get permission from your former employer to use it.)

Appendix A:
Accomplishments Portfolio Template

Accomplishments Portfolio

Your Name Here

Prepared for

Contact

Company Name

Contents

Tab 1: RÉSUMÉ

Tab 2: AWARDS

Tab 3: TESTIMONIALS

Tab 4: REFERENCES

Tab 5: CASE STUDIES

Tab 6: TRAINING

Tab 7: SKILLS PROFILE

Tab 8: QUALIFICATIONS

Appendix B:
Sales Training/New Business Development Programs, Keynotes, and Books Offered by Sittig Incorporated

Sales Training Programs

Sittig Incorporated is the developer of an activity-based sales training program called The Blitz Experience that empowers salespeople to schedule appointments with qualified prospects the day of the training, resulting in a pipeline full of new opportunities at the end of the day. This unique sales training program requires prospecting activity the day of the training so sales reps are actually filling their pipelines with new opportunities using the techniques taught during the training. Blitz Experience clients have reported increased sales of as much as 20 percent as a direct result of this innovative sales training program. Here is what Sittig Incorporated clients have to say about The Blitz Experience:

> *"ToolWatch Investment in The Blitz Experience: $7500.00*
> *Revenue Generated to Date from Blitz Leads: $79,011.76*
> *ROI: 10+×*
> *Thought you would like to know, the guys here appreciate you!!*
> *And of course you will always be my favorite Blitz Master!!!"*
> - Michael Norton, CEO and Founder, CanDoGo,
> Sales Consultant, ToolWatch

> *"In over thirty years of being responsible for showing return on investment for training programs, The Blitz Experience® is the FIRST training program that provides a means of easily connecting the results of the training to the bottom line. Level 4*

evaluation of training is what organizations strive to achieve with any employee development program—'Does the training effect the achievement of organizational goals?!' We have seen in only a few short weeks after the training that appointments were being made in places where 'we couldn't get arrested' before! Not surprisingly, many appointments are converting to orders—hooray!"

- Tom Kennedy, Vice President of Human Resources, SunSource

"One of the greatest benefits of learning a new skill and then putting it into action is the positive impact it has on your attitude. Knowing how to set great appointments will translate into energy and confidence on the phone. Your activity will increase, and because your skill has increased, so will your results. Does it work? I know it works! You see, not only have we trained thousands of salespeople through the years, we are also a customer of The Blitz Experience, and we have benefited from the skills and techniques taught in this program."

- Tom Ziglar, CEO, Ziglar Corporation

To learn more about these sales training programs, contact Sittig Incorporated at 206-769-4886, info@sittiginc.com, or visit www.sittiginc.com.

Keynotes

Ms. Sittig-Rolf delivers informative and entertaining keynote speeches on sales-related topics at sales conferences and corporate events, as well as association meetings. Choose from a variety of prepared keynotes, or have one customized especially for your event. Her animated and conversational style will engage your group immediately and will keep them learning and laughing throughout the presentation. Attendees of Ms. Sittig-Rolf's keynotes have said the following:

"Andrea, I wanted to say a big thanks for the great presentation you gave this morning! My colleague and I really enjoyed it and found your comments (and enthusiasm) extremely helpful!"
- Strategic Administration Specialist, agricultural products company

"Andrea, just wanted to say 'Thanks' for the presentation on Tuesday. Your attention-getting ideas will be most helpful. I'm looking forward to reading your book... I just skimmed the section on proposals and know there are ideas to make our proposals sizzle!"
- President, graphics design company

To learn more about the keynote offerings, contact Sittig Incorporated at 206-769-4886, info@sittiginc.com, or visit www.sittiginc.com.

Books

Ms. Sittig-Rolf is the author of three compelling sales books. The first, *Business-to-Business Prospecting: Innovative Techniques to Get Your Foot in the Door with Any Prospect* (Aspatore Books, 2005), is endorsed by best-selling author and sales guru Brian Tracy as well as Skip Miller, Steve Farber, and Ronald J. Walsh.

Her second is *The Seven Keys to Effective Business-to-Business Appointment Setting: Unlock Your Sales Potential* (Aspatore Books, 2006). The foreword is written by Tom Ziglar, CEO of the Ziglar Corporation, and it's endorsed by several sales gurus.

Her third book, *Power Referrals: The Ambassador Method for Empowering Others to Promote Your Business and Do the Selling for You* (McGraw-Hill, 2008), is endorsed by sales training gurus Tom Hopkins, Dr. Tony Alessandra, Michael Norton, and best-selling author of the *Selling to VITO* book series, Anthony Parinello.

Appendix C:
Free Sittig Incorporated Resources

Sales Tips Newsletter
sittiginc.com/free_resources.cfm

***Sales Solutions* Archives**
(from the *Puget Sound Business Journal*, 2004–2006)
sittiginc.com/free_resources.cfm

WomenEntreprenuer.com
Column: "Sales Blazer"
www.womenentrepreneur.com/columnist/754.html

CanDoGo
CanDoGo is a Web site with free expert advice from over 150 world-renowned authors, speakers, and trainers delivered in video, text, and audio format. The expert advice is short, concise, and helps you solve the issue at hand.
www.candogo.com

Sittig Professional Leads Network
The Sittig Professional Leads Network is a Twitter-enabled contact manager that generates free business leads for the successful business owner or sales professional. This simple Web-based service allows users to connect to our global network of trusted businesspeople, who provide you with unlimited qualified leads.
sittiginc.mywayinteractive.com

Downloads

Go to www.revyourresume.com and click on "Free Downloads" to get additional information to help you put into practice what you've learned from this book. When prompted for the password, enter "mydreamjob" to access the downloads.

About the Author

Andrea Sittig-Rolf helps organizations inspire change, maximize sales, and increase bottom-line results. Business-savvy with a passion for people, she understands how to help salespeople be their best and has what it takes to inspire them. She is a successful entrepreneur, author, and sales trainer, and is in high demand as a speaker and workshop leader.

Ms. Sittig-Rolf is the author of three compelling sales books called *Business-to-Business Prospecting: Innovative Techniques to Get Your Foot in the Door with Any Prospect* (Aspatore Books, 2005), endorsed by best-selling author and leading sales guru Brian Tracy; *The Seven Keys to Effective Business-to-Business Appointment Setting: Unlock Your Sales Potential* (Aspatore Books, 2006), endorsed and foreword written by Tom Ziglar, CEO of the Ziglar Corporation; and *Power Referrals: The Ambassador Method for Empowering Others to Promote Your Business and Do the Selling For You* (McGraw-Hill, 2008), endorsed by sales gurus Tom Hopkins, Dr. Tony Alessandra, Michael Norton, and Anthony Parinello, best-selling author of the *Selling to VITO* book series.

Ms. Sittig-Rolf is also the former host of the popular Internet radio talk show she created called "Power Talk: When Talent and Passion Collide, Success is Inevitable," where she interviewed guests such as *Mars vs. Venus* relationship guru Dr. John Gray, godfather of design television, Christopher Lowell, and best-selling author Marcus Buckingham. She is also a columnist for WomenEntrepreneur.com and has appeared on national television and radio shows across the United States.

Ms. Sittig-Rolf is an expert content provider for CanDoGo, a Web site with free expert advice from over 150 world-renowned authors, speakers, and trainers delivered in video, text, and audio format, found online at www.candogo.com. The expert advice is short, concise, and helps you solve the issue at hand. She is also an e-learning expert providing sales-related webinars for Business Expert Webinars, found online at www.businessexpertwebinars.com.

Ms. Sittig-Rolf is the founder and president of Sittig Incorporated, a sales training and consulting organization based in Redmond, Washington, found online at www.sittiginc.com. She is also the creator of The Blitz Experience, an activity-based new business development program that empowers salespeople to schedule appointments with qualified prospects the day of the training, resulting in a pipeline full of new opportunities at the end of the day.

Ms. Sittig-Rolf graduated from Southwest Texas State University in 1991 with a bachelor's degree in psychology. She lives in Redmond, Washington, with her husband, Brian.